EMPIRE INTO COMMONWEALTH

Empire into Commonwealth

THE CHICHELE LECTURES DELIVERED AT
OXFORD IN MAY 1960 ON 'CHANGES IN
THE CONCEPTION AND STRUCTURE OF THE
BRITISH EMPIRE DURING THE LAST HALF
CENTURY'

by

THE RT HON. EARL ATTLEE,
K.G., P.C., O.M., C.H.

London
OXFORD UNIVERSITY PRESS
NEW YORK
1961

Oxford University Press, Amen House, London E.C.4

GLASGOW NEW YORK TORONTO MELBOURNE WELLINGTON
BOMBAY CALCUTTA MADRAS KARACHI KUALA LUMPUR
CAPE TOWN IBADAN NAIROBI ACCRA

PRINTED IN GREAT BRITAIN

I

I HAVE had the honour of being invited to deliver this year's Chichele Historical Lectures and have chosen as my subject Changes in the Conception and Structure of the British Empire during the last half century.

There have been many great Empires in the history of the world that have risen, flourished for a time, and then fallen. Some on account of attack by a rival or by insurgent barbarians; some have decayed through internal weakness; while others have been resolved into a number of separate and contentious national States. There is only one Empire where, without external pressure or weariness at the burden of ruling, the ruling people has voluntarily surrendered its hegemony over subject peoples and has given them their freedom, where also the majority of the people so liberated have continued in political association with their former rulers. This unique example is the British Empire. The process of the transformation of an Empire into a Commonwealth, an association of free and equal States, has taken place during the last sixty years, a period which covers my adult life. I have seen it happen, and have taken some share in bringing it about.

I have no pretentions to be either an historian or a political scientist, but I have lived through this re-markable period, first as an ordinary citizen, later as a Member of Parliament and a Minister of the Crown. I have seen and felt the changes in the climate of opinion. I have known some of the leading personalities involved. The process is not yet complete, but it is not likely that the trend which has already gone so far will be reversed, for the developments which have taken place and are occurring today register a change in public opinion which is no less striking than the actual events.

I am in these lectures giving what is essentially a personal impression. They are not the result of research, but only of reflection. I shall not attempt to give any detailed examination of the niceties of constitutions or to trace the history of national movements, but I shall only try to paint a broad picture.

I shall begin my story with the British Empire at its apogee and in subsequent lectures discuss the developments of self-government. I shall not deal with the matter in strict chronological order, but speak first of the changes which took place in the parts of the Empire wholly or mainly inhabited by persons of European stock, secondly, of the changes in Asia, and lastly, of those in Africa or in regions inhabited by people of African stock. This does in some sort conform to chronology, for the movements to self-determination and independence begin among the Europeans, then extend to the Asians, and now are in full operation among the African people.

I shall take as my start Queen Victoria's Jubilee in 1897, which was a great parade of Empire just before the beginnings of change. I remember going up as a schoolboy and watching the procession. There was the old Queen with a great retinue of kings, many of them her descendants; there were Indian Princes, and there were carriages with Prime Ministers, not many of them —notably, I remember, the handsome figure of Sir Wilfred Laurier in his grey frock coat, the outstanding figure, the symbol of things to come. And then there followed the contingents of troops, black men, brown men, yellow men, white men from all parts of the far-flung empire, from every continent. They marched past paying tribute to their sovereign Queen, the little old lady who had ruled for sixty years. I remember going out in the evening and seeing the bonfires blazing on the hills.

It was a memorable day. It marked the highest point of imperialism. Most of us boys at that time were imperialists with an immense pride in the achievements of our race. It was curious that the one warning note against our overweening pride should have been struck by the chief popularizer of imperialism, Rudyard Kipling in his 'Recessional'.

Let us see, then, what was the composition of the Empire at that time, that great Empire ruled by the people of a little island, safe behind the guns of the British Fleet, which rode the seven seas unchallenged. It was essentially an empire built on sea power. The seas which separated other peoples united us. In Europe there was John Bull's other island, an unwilling member; the Isle of Man; and the Channel Islands. There were the three Mediterranean islands, Gibraltar, Malta, and Cyprus, with peoples of alien stock, useful little posts for the Navy like their Oriental counter-parts, Aden, Singapore, and Hong Kong. There were the lands which were really colonies, settled in the main by migrants from Britain—Canada, part-British, part-French; and Newfoundland, a maritime province which had remained outside the Canadian Federation and was a separate unit. There were the Caribbean colonies in the West Indian islands, and two colonies on the American mainland, British Guiana and British Honduras. All these had a European ruling class. On the other side of the world there were the Australian colonies as yet unfederated and New Zealand, counterparts of what we have seen in America, and a number of Pacific islands with dark-skinned inhabitants ruled by white men.

In Asia Queen Victoria as the successor of the Moguls was the Empress of India ruling directly or indirectly nearly three hundred million Asians. Burma had only recently been added to this Empire, but Ceylon was a separate colony. Farther East there was Malaya and Borneo and the great port of Singapore, and in the Far East the island of Hong Kong.

In South Africa there were the two colonies with settled European populations and larger numbers of Africans, while in East and West Africa were great tracts of territory inhabited by Africans—Nigeria, the Gold Coast, Sierra Leone—recently acquired in what has been described as the scramble for Africa, but recorded in the dates which I learnt at school under the more decorous title of 'The European powers begin to arrange their spheres of influence in Africa'. In central Africa the Chartered Company was pushing northwards to create Rhodesia. Finally, in North Africa

4

Britain and Egypt had just completed the reconquest of the Sudan.

So at that time nearly a quarter of the globe owed allegiance to the widow of Windsor. The trader and the missionary over the years had carried British influence and rule all over the world.

Lord Salisbury, who had succeeded a Liberal imperialist Lord Rosebery at the head of a Conservative administration, was in power in Britain and held the doctrine of splendid isolation. Britain ruled the seas and regarded herself as entitled to pursue her own course with a benevolent interest in the affairs of other nations not so fortunate. Joseph Chamberlain, the apostle of imperialism, was at the Colonial Office. He was teaching the British people to think imperially. He told them what was their rôle in the world. It was to rule other races who had not the privileges that belonged to the British. Kipling was the prophet of Empire with a great influence over the young, the banjo bard of the British Empire, as a Frenchman of the time called him.

Cecil Rhodes, with his dream of an African empire extending from the Cape to Cairo, characteristically combined a political vision with moneymaking on a great scale. His reputation had indeed been sullied and his career checked by the tragi-comedy of the Jameson raid. How well I remember my father reading the account of this at the breakfast-table shortly before my twelfth birthday. My father was a Gladstonian Liberal and a lawyer and was shocked at this breach of the law, but to us Dr Jim was a hero. In India there was

Lord Curzon in the viceregal chair, the most magnificent and imperial of Viceroys. Egypt, though an independent State, was unobtrusively ruled in the interest of the bondholders by Lord Cromer. Britain and Egypt had just smashed the fanatical dervishes, won back the Sudan for civilization, and inaugurated that interesting experiment which has only recently terminated, tersely described as the rule of blacks by Blues. In Africa Lugard and others were working out the experiment of indirect rule whereby the British preserved law and order while Africans were left as far as possible to the direct rule of their Chiefs administering their native laws and customs.

On the wall at school hung a great map with large portions of it coloured red. It was an intoxicating vision for a small boy, for, as we understood it, all these people were ruled for their own good by strong silent men, civil servants and soldiers as portrayed by Kipling. We believed in our great imperial mission. We knew little of the seamy side of empire, of the financiers and dubious characters behind our empire builders. Hilaire Belloc was to enlighten us later.

The British Empire was an extension of Britain. At home the ruling classes enjoyed a high standard of life while the masses were poor. The capitalists pursued profit-making while the State looked after law and order. Abroad, as at home, there was an admirable and honest civil service, and there were clergy at home like the missionaries abroad to call attention to other values. The Empire was a great field for exploitation by the capitalists, while for the younger sons of the better-fed classes it offered a great opportunity for service.

It is well to remember that despite much vulgar ostentation and the exploitation of backward peoples, there was this other side which appealed to adventurous and idealistic youth. There were hundreds of men giving devoted service and hard and honest work to the task of bringing civilization to primitive or backward peoples. They lived and not infrequently died prematurely in unpleasant conditions. They set a high standard of devotion to duty and to honest administration in the interest of the governed. Countries that have now become self-governing have profited much from their work and example.

Britain was not alone in the colonial field. It was the age of Empire. France and Belgium, Holland and Portugal had their empires, and late entrants such as Germany and Italy strove to follow the prevailing fashion.

Another vivid memory of that time. I was going up for my school entrance examination. My master gave me an illustrated paper. I recall the picture on the front page of the defeat of the Italians by King Menelik at Adowa. I little thought then that later we would be concerned at the attempt of Mussolini to realize the dreams of Crispi.

It confirmed our opinion that, generally speaking, other people were not so good at the game as we were. There were scandals in the Congo. There were stories of the brutality of the Germans to the Hereros. We had clashed with the French when Major Marchand made his historic expedition across the Sahara to try to anticipate us in the Sudan. It was the day of imperialism. Europeans ruled the world. Apart, of course, from the people of the United States, whom we regarded more or less as honorary Europeans, all over the world Europeans were dominant. Europeans tended to take over any odd pieces of territory, the inhabitants of which could not defend themselves and which seemed to offer opportunities for profit.

It is to be remembered that at that time the British Empire was a free trade empire. Our dependencies were open to the traders of other nations, while we had all the expenses of acquiring them and ruling them. So why, we thought, should anyone object?

Outside the great European powers, there were only two other great countries: the United States of America and Russia. They were engaged in consolidating continents. That, of course, was not imperialism. The essence of imperialism is crossing the sea; gradually extending one's rule and mopping up a whole continent is not imperialism but manifest destiny. There were two other old empires at the time, those of Spain and Portugal, but they were rather moribund we thought.

Well, there was our Empire, and Britain ruled over all these territories. They were governed from Whitehall. We had, it was true, been wise enough after what happened in the eighteenth century in America to concede self-government to Europeans in Canada, Australia, and New Zealand. There was no idea whatever at that time of handing over power to Asians and Africans. Indeed, why should the rulers of Britain give

8

the franchise to what Kipling called 'the lesser breeds without the law' when they denied it to a considerable section of men in their own country and to all women?

There was another great country which did not at that time play much of a part in the world, and that was China. It was nibbled at by European powers. Its sovereignty was infringed by treaties of one kind and another, and small pieces of it were bitten off. There were a few independent states—Afghanistan, Siam, Persia, and Ethiopia. There was a pleasing term used for them; they were regarded as 'buffer states', something interposed between the rival ambitious and quarrelsome Europeans. There was only one exception to European dominance and that was Japan, which we thought was rather an Asian counterpart of ourselves. They had recently defeated China and were soon to defeat Russia. They were so good at war that they were regarded as almost honorary Europeans.

That was the position in 1897. But the next few years were to be pregnant with change. There were two major events, the South African War and the Russo-Japanese War. The South African War was the first war for many years where the British had to meet Europeans. I recall it very well because had I been a little bigger I might well have served in it, as did many of my school contemporaries. As it was, I was only caned for excessive patriotism. Here was something new in our experience. An attempt to bring a people of European stock by force into the Empire. I don't intend here to tell the story of how in defence of what we schoolboys believed the cause of freedom we fought two little reactionary South African republics. We had the delusion at that time that the rather unsavoury cosmopolitan clique of financiers in Johannesburg stood for freedom and democracy, and we cheerfully joined up to fight.

Field Marshal Smuts often said to me that the South African War was the beginning of the end of imperialism. I think he was right. Many results flowed from this war. We may note that it had its effect on the relationship between Britain and Germany. The Kaiser, who had sent messages of goodwill and a notorious telegram to President Kruger, was much annoyed when he found that owing to the British Fleet he was impotent to take any more effective action, and accordingly Admiral Tirpitz was set to work to build a German Fleet. The campaign showed up the military weakness of Britain. This rather outraged German opinion. The Germans saw right without might, a thing quite contrary to their philosophy.

The South African War made Britain extremely unpopular on the Continent of Europe. There was much self-righteous talk of this wicked invasion of the rights of small nations. It worsened our relations with the United States, then entering on an imperial phase themselves at the expense of a decadent Spain, but that was, of course, inspired by the loftiest motives.

But another important result had its effect on the Empire. It brought colonial contingents into the field. Some years before, imperial troops had been withdrawn from the self-governing Dominions and some small local forces had been enrolled, for it is axiomatic that imperial troops cannot be put under the orders of any government than that of Whitehall. There were, however, very effective volunteer contingents from the overseas dominions taking part in the South African War. There was also, curiously enough, a volunteer ambulance section from India raised and commanded by Mr Gandhi.

Still more important was the revolt against imperialism which followed the termination of the war. There had always been protests against the cruder exhibitions of colonial exploitation. There were Little Englanders. There were meetings at Exeter Hall, where the non-conformist conscience became vocal. There were also the few socialists. All these people were regarded with contempt; and although the abolition of the slave trade had evoked great enthusiasm in Britain and much had been done by the British Government in its suppression, less-direct forms of exploitation were not generally condemned. In the course of building up the Empire it was the habit to import labour for the exploitation of rich territories from anywhere where it was most convenient. It was notable that one of these efforts, that of the introduction of Chinese labour into the Rand gold-mines in Africa, was one of the major factors in turning the nation against imperialism. One may note here that our Empire builders naturally did not foresee the time when Africans and Asians would demand and be given the right of self-government. The habit of importing labour left many problems to their successors of today. It resulted in mixed communities, as in Malaya, where you have the Chinese, the Malays, and the Indians; and in Fiji and elsewhere, where there were Indian importations. But it was a time when labour was still regarded mainly as one of the factors in production. It was natural that there should be a complete disregard of the long-term problems created in the pursuit of profit.

The South African War did much to discredit imperialism, and its aftermath was the great Liberal victory of 1906, which shall be dealt with in due course.

The other major event was Japan's defeat of Russia. For many years no Asiatic power had successfully challenged the Europeans; not since the Turks were driven back from the walls of Vienna had there been any real challenge of the Europeans—though one may doubt if Tsarist Russia was really a European power; it was rather an Asian power with a thin veneer of European civilization. It counted as one of the great powers of Europe, and its defeat by Japan made a profound impression. I would trace from that victory of Japan the beginnings of Asianism. Asia began to awake. No longer was it true that 'she let the legions thunder past and plunged in thought again'. Asians began to question why they should be ruled by Europeans. Japan's victory gave them self-confidence. The results were long delayed, but they came in full measure in due time.

II

In this lecture I propose to deal with those parts of the British Empire which are either inhabited by people of European stock or are predominantly so. While there were certain small territories that came under the rule of the Home Office, before 1925 all colonies, whether self-governing or not, came under the Colonial Office. It was not till later that a separate office, first called the Dominions Office and later the Commonwealth Relations Office, was established. At the beginning of the century the Colonial Office, the importance of which had been greatly exalted by the dynamic personality of Joseph Chamberlain, ruled over the major part of the Empire.

Canada was then the most advanced. It is not my purpose in these lectures to deal with earlier history, but reference must be made to the famous Durham Report, from which sprang the great constitutional advance in Canada, and the creation of the Dominion under the leadership of Sir John Macdonald. Canada was by far the most important part of the self-governing colonies, though the West was not developed. Alberta, Manitoba, Saskatchewan had still to come into existence. It was notable that in Canada there was a great French-speaking population, and at the end of the nineteenth century for the first time a French-speaking Canadian, Sir Wilfred Laurier, was the Prime Minister. Australia was not yet federated. It was a group of small colonies, all of them self-governing, but they were not united till 1901. New Zealand was a small unitary state, while little Newfoundland, with a population of only 300,000, ranked as fully self-governing. But foreign policy and major defence were still imperial. The will of the Empire was located in Whitehall.

To these old self-governing colonies there was added the Union of South Africa. The two colonies and the two former Boer republics were united. This was effected by the Liberal Government of 1906. The Boers had only just been defeated, and to hand over South Africa to what would almost certainly be a predominantly Boer electorate was a great act of faith. It was the major achievement of Sir Henry Campbell-Bannerman in his short Premiership; and to him must go the credit, for it is generally agreed that it was his initiative that forced the measure through the Cabinet. But equal credit must be given to the Boer leaders, General Botha and General Smuts.

Here indeed were two great and broad-minded men. Smuts indeed was to become one of the greatest of Commonwealth statesmen while Botha's action in the First World War and Smuts's in the Second defeated the efforts of the Germans and some Boers to help or at least not to oppose the Kaiser and Hitler. It is a remarkable feature of the Commonwealth that many of its Prime Ministers have either fought against or have been imprisoned by the British. I have myself presided at the Conference Table where sat Mr Mackenzie King, whose proud boast it was that his grandfather Lyon Mackenzie had had a price put on his head as a rebel by the British Government, Marshal Smuts, who fought against us in the Boer War, and Mr Nehru, who was imprisoned by the Indian Government many times. The precedent is followed, for Mr Nkrumah has been imprisoned and Archbishop Makarios deported.

The two colonies and the two former republics were united to form the Union of South Africa. This indeed was liberalism in action. But even liberalism in those days did not extend to giving political rights to persons of non-European stock, whether Africans, coloured people, or Indians. In the debates on the legislation in the House of Commons some Labour and Radical Members, such as Keir Hardie and Sir Charles Dilke, raised the question of proper protection for the Africans. But the House as a whole did not seem to realize the danger in giving complete political power to a white minority of employers.

The precedent set here was extended to Rhodesia in 1923. Rhodesia had been ruled by the Chartered Company of which Cecil Rhodes was the presiding genius. It was the last of these politico-economic companies, of which the greatest was the East India Company, where power was given to a commercial undertaking to rule people of alien stock. There was, however, one difference in the case of Rhodesia, for power was retained by the Imperial Government, though seldom if ever exercised, to disallow legislation considered by the home Government to be inequitable as between white and black.

But before Rhodesia obtained its position of being almost a fully self-governing dominion great events were to take place. In 1901 the colonies in Australia agreed to federate, which resulted in the formation of the Commonwealth of Australia and in fact in the creation of an Australian nation. In 1914 there came the First World War. Here for the first time on a major scale fighting men from the Dominions made a big contribution to victory. Today Australia and New Zealand look back at Anzac as a decisive stage of their development into full nationhood. During that war for the first time colonial statesmen were called in to take part in decisions of policy. They sat in the British Cabinet. General Smuts was a full member of the British Government. In fact, these Dominions appeared as full and independent nations. As such they participated in the Peace Conference and obtained full membership of the League of Nations. South Africa accepted a mandate for South-West Africa, as did Australia for New Guinea and Samoa, and New Zealand for sundry islands.

It was quite clear by the end of that war that the status of the white colonies had changed. No longer could they be ruled from Whitehall. They had become nations. There had formerly been Imperial Conferences, but there was no doubt who was the master at these assemblies. But in 1926 a new note was struck and the white colonies become Dominions. They were defined as follows: 'Dominions are autonomous communities within the British Empire in no way subordinate to one another in domestic and external affairs though united together by common allegiance to the Crown and freely associated as members of the

British Commonwealth of Nations.' This change, already a fact, was put into legal form by the Statute of Westminster, which was passed in 1931. I can recall this very well, as I was at that time a Minister and was detailed to assist the Prime Minister, Mr Ramsay MacDonald, at the Imperial Conference.

There was implicit in this declaration the right of secession. As equal members and in no way subordinate to one another, it was clear that there could be no power to prevent any member from leaving if it should so decide. It was as a matter of fact this feature of the Statute of Westminster that raised the very strong opposition of Sir Winston Churchill. It must also have puzzled the people of the United States, who fought a great war just to prevent this right of secession. It was used first by Eire and later by Burma; and one might perhaps add by the Sudan, though the Sudan's membership of the Empire was always a little doubtful owing to the condominium with Egypt.

One might note here the position of Eire or Southern Ireland. Southern Ireland had been a part of Great Britain, and theoretically therefore was a partner in governing the Empire, but she had always accepted this rôle unwillingly and had demanded home rule. The First World War saw an Irish rebellion and a long and bloody struggle which eventually resulted in Southern Ireland obtaining her independence. It was only too characteristic of the ways of imperialists that eventually a predominantly Conservative Government had to concede to Michael Collins, the rebel, what they had refused to Redmond, the constitutional statesman. One may note that this precedent obtains even at the present day when a Conservative Government has had to concede self-government to Archbishop Makarios after having condemned him and exiled him for two years, and after two years of guerilla warfare. Ireland, however, for a time accepted a somewhat anomalous position in which she did still belong to the Commonwealth, until somewhat lightheartedly Mr Costello broke the last link, thereby digging even deeper the ditch between Northern and Southern Ireland. But the anomalies continue, and today while Southern Ireland is a foreign country, her citizens can come over here, can obtain employment, and can vote in elections. It has never been possible to apply logical rules to Ireland.

Meanwhile let us consider the progress in other parts of the Empire. Newfoundland has had a somewhat chequered history. Although non-viable economically, she was raised to the full status of a dominion, but owing to bad economic conditions and a corrupt government, she was eventually obliged to surrender her sovereignty and was treated by the Conservative British Government of the day rather as if she had been a defaulting Board of Guardians. A Commission of Government was put in and she ceased to be a self-governing Dominion. However, her sailors and soldiers took a full part in the Second World War, and I was at the time Dominions Secretary. I took the occasion to visit that country, the first Minister to do so, and reviewed the situation. It was clear to me that the future of Newfoundland was bound up with her greater neighbour, Canada. A former attempt to bring her into the Dominion had failed, but a year or two after the end of the Second World War a plebiscite was held and Newfoundland became one of the provinces of Canada.

The future of Rhodesia had better be treated perhaps in Lecture IV, when I deal with some of the problems of the African continent.

Cyprus, obtained by Mr Disraeli as part of the general settlement made at the Treaty of Berlin, had been treated as a Crown Colony, but the demand for self-determination, which is an inevitable concomitant, it seems, of world wars, led her to demand not independence but union with Greece. The situation was difficult and complicated because, while the majority of the population speak Greek and are attracted to their co-linguists, there is a section of Turks. The whole position too was bedevilled by strategic considerations. It is very difficult for a small country with a divided population to settle down as a single unit, particularly in the Middle East, where toleration is not a notable feature in human relationships. Since the delivery of these lectures, a settlement has now been arrived at.

Malta, again too small to be viable economically, being really a British dockyard town with a small hinterland, offered another problem. The Prime Minister, Mr Mintoff, made a suggestion that Malta should be united to Britain and should be represented in the House of Commons. This seemed to me at the time a most hopeful suggestion, and it was accepted by a joint committee of Lords and Commons. But unfortunately Mr Mintoff and his friends pressed for too heavy commitments by Britain in the financial and economic sphere, and the future therefore is still uncertain.

There are some other small parts of the Empire inherited by Britain, curious anachronisms. The Isle of Man has a very ancient parliament and is self-governing, although every year its Customs Bill has to be passed by the House of Commons. But no difficulty seems to have arisen from the fact that this little island governs herself. Yet another anomaly is the Channel Islands, the remains of the old Duchy of Normandy. There again you have a very small population governing itself; its immediate relations with the British Government are through the Home Office, but no question ever seems to have arisen of its right to govern itself. And so far no demand for self-government has come from Gibraltar, which after all is only a small fortress.

Let us now look back to the general relationship of the European-inhabited dominions. We may note the gradual disappearance of certain uniting factors. In the old Empire all parts of the Empire owed allegiance to the British monarch, but this uniformity was broken, first by Eire, which proclaimed itself a republic, and later by India and Pakistan, and it is a question as to how long this link will remain in South Africa. Formerly Governors and Governor-Generals were appointed by the Crown on the advice of the British Prime Minister, but after the First World War it was agreed, as part, so to speak, of the coming-of-age of the dominions, that henceforward with these appointments the Crown should act on the advice of the Prime Minister of the Dominion concerned. Undoubtedly the old practice gave a certain close link. I remember that King George VI said to me how valuable he found it to have people around him whom he would meet who had been Governor-Generals or Governors in the Dominions. Today it is open to the Prime Minister of any of the Dominions to recommend for appointment anyone, whether from his own Dominion or another. A further link used to be the Judicial Committee of the Privy Council, the supreme authority administering many different codes of law. Canada was the first to exercise the right to do away with the appeal to the Privy Council. It was, I think, a pity, because while one of the great binding ties throughout the British Commonwealth is a common respect for the rule of law, and especially respect for the British common law, a supreme tribunal on which sat judges of the highest distinction from the various countries of the Commonwealth was, I think, a matter of some importance. Formerly, of course, long distances to travel made for great expense, but nowadays with the advent of air travel much of this is saved. Indeed, it would be quite possible to have a peripatetic tribunal sitting from time to time in different parts of the Commonwealth.

At this point I must call attention to the great influence of the law as a stimulus to the desire for self-government and as a unifying factor in the Commonwealth. The practice of the law has always had a great attraction both for Indians and other races living in the Empire. Despite self-government, you will still see that in the Calls to the Bar half of the names are of students from overseas, and this has obtained for years.

I recall the story of my old master in the law, Theo Mathew, a great wit. Walking up the library of the Middle Temple, he found every bay occupied by Indians or Africans until, at the far end, he espied one English student. He dashed up to him, shook him by the hand, and said, 'Dr Livingstone, I presume!'

Learning the history of the rule of law in Britain, the student could not help being aware of the gulf between the British system of Government and colonial rule. Magna Carta and the Bill of Rights, Habeas Corpus, and the position of the Crown and the people were lively incentives to young men from overseas. One cannot imagine rulers of other Empires such as Germany or Russia being blind to the dangers of exposing youth to such influences.

Most of the leaders of the movement for self-government in India were called to the English Bar. Today in the Commonwealth the acceptance of the broad principles of the English common law is a great unifying influence.

The Second World War again showed great changes in the Commonwealth but during the war there was, I think, far closer contact kept with the Dominions. As the war extended to the Far East it was quite clear that there must be the closest possible consultation with the Governments of Australia and New Zealand; in fact, there were visits from those Prime Ministers, and when present in London they sat in the Cabinet. And naturally owing to their great increase of population and wealth, the Dominions took a greater part in the Second World War than they did in the First World War. Similarly, in the San Francisco Conference which resulted in the creation of U.N.O., Commonwealth representatives were very prominent, particularly Field Marshal Smuts. I was a member of the British delegation to San Francisco, and every morning I would preside at meetings of the Commonwealth representatives; no binding decisions were taken, but there was very full consultation. Indeed, there were differences: Peter Fraser of New Zealand was always a very strong opponent of the veto, which the British delegation were obliged to support.

Before proceeding to deal with the extension of full self-government to Asian and African peoples, I should like to deal a little with the organization of the Commonwealth. This, I think, is an appropriate point in these lectures to deal with this, because the methods built up in the old Commonwealth did not alter when it became multi-racial. The first point about the Commonwealth is that, as one might expect from a British creation, it has no constitution and it has no rules. From time to time suggestions are made that it should be a more definite structure, but so far these have not been accepted. In its essence it is an organization of completely independent units and there is no power to coerce any one of them. The Commonwealth Relations Office, as the old Dominions Office is now called, is entirely different from the Colonial Office. The Secretary of State for the Colonies administered great countries; the Secretary of State for Commonwealth Relations is much more analogous to the Foreign Secretary, although—as to be truly British there must be an anomaly—he does administer the three protectorates in South Africa, Basutoland, Swaziland and Bechuanaland. Commonwealth representatives, whether in other dominions or abroad, rank as Ambassadors, although in the Commonwealth we prefer to call them High Commissioners. Only in the last few years were High Commissioners given the same status as Ambassadors; in fact, the relationship of a High Commissioner to the Governor in the Commonwealth country to which he is accredited is far more intimate than that of an Ambassador, even where there is a very close alliance. This was particularly notable during the Second World War. When I was Secretary of State for the Dominions I would meet the High Commissioners every morning to give them all the latest information and to discuss any problems that might arise. And there is a constant flow of communications between the Secretary of State in Britain and Commonwealth Governments.

From time to time meetings of Prime Ministers, or occasionally of Ministers of External Affairs or Finance Ministers, take place. The most important of these is that of Prime Ministers. It is, of course, a very difficult thing to get a time, having regard to differences of climate and distances to travel, to assemble all the Prime Ministers. This was done pretty successfully in the War and subsequently. I recall my first Commonwealth conference, when as Chancellor of the Duchy of

Lancaster and maid-of-all-work in the Government, I assisted Mr Ramsay MacDonald at the conference in 1931. It is my impression that proceedings then were more formal than subsequently; I seem to recall only two primary meetings of Prime Ministers, while the rest of the work was done in committees and sub-committees and informal gatherings. In my own time the most important part of a Commonwealth gathering was the meetings of Prime Ministers without officials. Behind the scenes the officials of the various departments are no doubt busy with details, but the essential feature of a Commonwealth meeting is a talk round the table between friends. There is seldom a very formal agenda. There is not even a formal calling of each Prime Minister in order of precedence to give his views; it was my practice when a subject came up to ask a Prime Minister who I thought was specially qualified to deal with the subject to open; thereafter discussions proceeded, but no vote was ever taken. As in a British Cabinet meeting, one arrived at a consensus of opinion. There are generally some inter-dominion difficulties, either unimportant or large, but it is not the practice to discuss these at formal meetings. In my time there was the very grave difficulty between Pakistan and India over Kashmir; the matter was never raised at a formal meeting, but a vast amount of time was taken up, both by me and by other Commonwealth Prime Ministers, in endeavouring to reach a settlement. Recently despite the dispute between South Africa and other members of the Commonwealth, the matter was fully ventilated, but outside the conference room.

Another very important link in the Commonwealth is the Commonwealth Parliamentary Association, under whose auspices Parliamentarians are brought together when visiting other member countries and in periodic conferences. It is not enough to have meetings of Ministers only. It is good that members of the legislatures, whether Government or opposition, should get to know each other. The legislatures of all the Dominions follow the pattern of that which sits at Westminster, and members and officials alike come to Westminster to study procedure.

The conferences are less important for the actual business done than for the opportunities they afford for members of Parliament of various races to form friendships and to understand each others' problems. I had the advantage of attending the conference last year in Canberra and saw myself how great was the unity achieved. All racial prejudices disappeared.

Foreigners find it difficult to understand how such loose methods can be effective, but the answer is that they are. I would not pretend to prophesy with regard to the future of the Commonwealth, but I think it unlikely that there will ever be evolved a written constitution or that a power of decision will be given. When one realizes that many members have only recently achieved full independence, it is not likely that they will readily surrender what they have gained.

It is interesting to note that differences of political allegiance never in my time arose at Commonwealth Conferences. My relations with Mr Menzies and Mr Sydney Holland were as cordial as those with Mr

Chiffley and Mr Peter Fraser, though the former were not and the latter were of my own political creed. Nor do I ever recall a division of opinion on racial grounds.

One great advantage of these conferences is that those participating can see international problems from various angles. The problems of South-East Asia appear different to the man who views them from a geographical position in Oceania and the man whose natural view is through the Mediterranean and the Suez canal.

III

At the dawn of the century the Indian Empire was by far the most populous of all countries under the British Crown. The possession of India dominated our strategy. Gibraltar, Malta, and Aden were stations on the way to India, while our dominant position in Egypt was largely due to our interests in the Suez Canal, through which went the shortest route between Britain and our Asiatic possessions. Lord Curzon, the great imperialist and Viceroy, staged a demonstration in the Delhi durbar which might be comparable to the '97 Jubilee. It was a great parade before change. There were all the Indian rulers and troops, both British and Indian. Here in India we had a whole continent ruled by an alien race. It is not my purpose to deal with the history of how our rule in India was built up or with the transfer of the old East India Company's possessions to the Crown, nor would I deal with the most recent acquisition, that of Burma; but there in 1900 one had nearly 300 million people, the larger part under the direct rule of the British, though there were very many who were under the government of their own Indian rulers. These Indian states, some 600 in number, ranged from Hyderabad with a population of nearly 15 million down to little chiefdoms of a few square miles. The Viceroy exercised sovereignty over these Indian states. On occasions rulers were deposed. In the major states there were British Residents who saw to it that the rulers did not stray outside the bounds of British policy. Some states, such as Mysore and Travancore, were as advanced as any part of British India; others, particularly in the hills, were extremely primitive. At the head of the administration was the Viceroy, responsible to the home Government, where there was the Secretary of State for India with his council of distinguished ex-civil servants.

Looking back at the past, you will find that our early rulers, men such as Sir Thomas Munro, Metcalfe, or Sir Henry Lawrence, never envisaged that British rule would endure for all time. They conceived that sooner or later Indians would want to rule themselves. But in the latter years of the nineteenth century it seemed that the British had really begun to see themselves as the top caste in this caste-ridden country. And indeed where anything like nationalist sentiment made itself felt it was apt to be regarded as sedition. India, being divided into peoples speaking many languages and adhering to various religions, had really been brought together only by the British. The first big nationalist movement arose under Lord Curzon's Viceroyalty, when for administrative reasons he proposed to partition the enormous province of Bengal; this roused Bengal nationalism, and for the first time there was something like a popular movement. Meanwhile there was a nationalist movement, led in the main by Indians who had received their education in Britain. In particular, there were numbers of lawyers who had received their training in the Inns of Court, while many had also been at Oxford and Cambridge. These

naturally carried back to India the ideas of freedom and
self-government that they found in Britain. A number
of them served in the higher grades of the civil service,
which was, of course, staffed in the lower ranks entirely
by Indians.

When the Liberals came into power in 1906 the
Secretary of State for India was John Morley, a rather
old-fashioned Radical, and while he certainly never
contemplated an India entirely governed by Indians,
he did institute some very partial reforms with the
object of associating the Indians in the government of
their own country. These are known as the Morley–
Minto Reforms—Lord Minto was the Viceroy. There
were some elections to local bodies, and these were
based on communal representation. It is as well to
glance at this, because it brings up at once the great
difficulty of establishing full self-government in India.
Hindus and Moslems were the chief rival communities;
now and again there had been riots between them,
particularly when their festivals clashed. While both
were alike under British rule this rivalry was subdued,
but as soon as the prospect of attaining power emerged
the relations between the two communities were
exacerbated. The Morley–Minto Reforms did not
amount to very much. It was a very tentative step.
There were some Indians introduced into the Indian
civil service. An Indian, Lord Sinha, was the first
Indian to serve on the Viceroy's Council, and there
were stirrings of nationalist unrest.

With the outbreak of the First World War India
automatically became a belligerent, and Indian troops

played a very big part, not only in the East in Meso-
potamia and Palestine but also on the Western Front.
When the Peace Conference at Paris was called there
were Indian representatives along with those of the
dominions. This was the first step in the recognition of
India as something more than a mere British possession.

Meanwhile a Liberal Secretary of State for India,
Mr Edwin Montagu, was conferring with the Viceroy,
Lord Chelmsford, for a further step in reform. There
was a declaration of aims in the Montagu–Chelmsford
Report. There was to be training in responsibility, but
there was to be a partnership in administration. This
scheme was known as 'dyarchy' and was, I believe, in-
vented by the distinguished Fellow of All Souls, Mr
Lionel Curtis. Under this scheme law and order and
finance, and of course defence and foreign affairs,
remained with the British, while the pleasanter departments—social service, education, and the rest—were
handed to Indians. Indians were also introduced into
the central Government and into the legislature. It was
almost a perfect training in irresponsibility. The unpleasant part of government remained with the British,
the pleasanter part with the Indians. However, where it
was worked, and in some places it was worked with
considerable success, it was a valuable training both in
administration and in parliament. I should mention
that already there had been a considerable amount of
local self-government, though in fact the civil servants'
decision generally carried the sway. There was also
sent out the Lee Commission with the object of speeding
up Indianization of the civil services. Very important

results followed from this: first of all the number of British administrators was steadily reduced, but there was a tendency to transfer British personnel to difficult districts, with the result that there was less and less contact with the masses. Formerly a civil servant might stay for years in a district and become almost the father of the people. In 1927 I asked the Bombay Government the average length of service in one district of the British administrator. The answer was nine months. It is worthwhile contrasting this with the practice in Indonesia and French Indo-China, where there was no attempt made to bring Asians into the higher ranks of the administration.

Meanwhile India became a prey to great agitation. On the side of the Hindus a remarkable leader appeared in the person of Mahatma Gandhi, who preached non-violent resistance to British rule. Mr Gandhi had many effective campaigns, although not infrequently some Indians departed from his principles, with results which he deplored. I think that it should be recalled that civil disobedience was possible in India because the Indian Government did not resort to ruthlessness. If Indian students lay down on a railway track as a demonstration the train stopped and the demonstrators were removed. The officers of a Hitler or a Stalin would have driven straight on. The one example of frightfulness, the shooting down of demonstrators in Amritsar, caused a violent reaction in England, and the General responsible was censured and retired.

At the same time there was a strong agitation in the ranks of the Moslems owing to the deposition of the

Sultan of Turkey. The mainly Hindu Congress movement worked at this time quite closely with the Moslem Khilafat movement. The appetite grew with the eating. Every concession to Indian nationalism set up new demands. It had been provided under the Montagu–Chelmsford scheme that there should be a review of the whole position after a term of years. In 1927 Mr Baldwin decided that the time had come for this review, and a Commission was set up under the chairmanship of Sir John Simon, known as the Simon Commission, of which I was appointed a member, on the grounds, I think, that I had a virgin mind on the subject.

The Commission worked for two years visiting all parts of India, but owing to the failure of the British Government to take fully into account Indian sentiment, it was boycotted by the Congress Party on the grounds that such a Commission should have contained Indians. This Commission reviewed the whole of the situation and made a number of recommendations. One was the separation of Burma, the Burmese being racially and traditionally quite distinct from the races of the Indian peninsula. Other recommendations were for the transfer of law and order in the provinces and a general quickening up of the tempo of advance. But the Commission was forced to withhold their agreement with the demand of the Indians for full dominion status. There were two main difficulties. One was the position of the Indian States; under treaties and sanads the Government of India was bound to uphold the Indian rulers, and there was already a considerable agitation among their subjects for more democratic constitutions and even for the merging of the States in British India. It would therefore have been quite impossible at that time to make British India a dominion while retaining the obligation to protect the Indian states.

It is axiomatic that where full self-government is attained by a member of the Commonwealth the state must be prepared to look after its own internal security and its external defence. India, which had always been faced with a difficult and restless North-West Frontier, was defended by the Army in India, which consisted partly of British troops, partly of Indian troops commanded by British officers; only a very few Indian commissioned officers had yet been appointed, and there was at that time no Indian officer of field rank. It would therefore have been impossible to hand over the defence of India to the Indians, nor would it have been possible to have handed over the protection of the Indian states to an Indian Army under the control of an Indian administration. There was besides a great communal tension, not only between Moslem and Hindu but also in Madras between Brahmin and non-Brahmin, and in Bombay between Gujeratis and Marathas; while all over India were the depressed classes who had practically no rights and the Anglo-Indian community, which looked for its way of living to subordinate services, especially on the railways. The Simon Commission was therefore unable to recommend an immediate handing over of power at the centre, though it proposed that there should be a federal organization between the Indian states and British India. As a member of that Commission it was quite clear to me that the possibilities of advance of a nation by the action of administrators of an alien race were limited. Most of the evils from which India suffered could not be dealt with without impinging on customs and ways of life bound up in religion. In earlier days the British had dealt with Suttee and Thuggee, but they could not deal with such matters as child marriage and family limitation or even with the discrimination against the untouchables. Only Indians could deal with these things. The question was how and when Indians should attain full self-government. It was clear that the Simon Report did not meet nationalist demands, though the Viceroy, Lord Halifax, recommended a declaration in favour of dominion status.

The next act in the drama was the summoning of a round-table conference to which, thanks to Lord Halifax, Mahatma Gandhi came. But despite much good will and discussion the conference broke down, largely on communal tension. The National Government that came into power in 1931, finding that the round-table conference method had failed, set up a joint select committee of Lords and Commons to make recommendations. In effect their recommendations followed the Simon Report in giving provincial self-government but delaying self-government at the centre until India was able to defend itself and until more agreement could be reached. This was followed by the introduction of the Government of India Act of 1935, which was piloted through the House of Commons with great skill by Sir Samuel Hoare against violent and obstructive opposition by Sir Winston Churchill and a handful of Conservatives. Lord Halifax subsequently went on record that without this opposition by Sir Winston Churchill and his friends we might perhaps have got an all-India solution to the Indian problem before the Second World War. Meanwhile, although there was a considerable amount of boycott, the 1935 Act was worked in the provinces with considerable success, though the advent of Hindu ministries had the effect of exacerbating Moslem opinion.

When the Second World War came, India—unwisely, I think—was brought into the War without any consultation with the leading Indian statesmen. And while the Indian armed forces for the most part, and the masses in India, were in full support of the Allies in the war against Fascism, politicians stood aloof and their leaders were sent to prison. The loss of so many possessions in Asia to Japan made a profound impression in India, and particularly when Burma was overrun. A few Indians, like a few Burmans, went so far as to try to help the victory of Japan under the delusion that a Japanese victory would bring them freedom, but closer contact with the Japanese very soon disillusioned them. As in the First World War, the fighting men of India took a very full part in the long struggle for victory.

Meanwhile there were discussions in the war-time Cabinet as to what was to be the future of India. It was realized that the need for action would be immediate after the War. It was agreed that Sir Stafford

Cripps, a personal friend of Mr Jawaharlal Nehru, who was now coming forward as the leader in India, should go out and meet Indian politicians and try to seek agreement. After much patient discussion the Cripps mission failed, largely due to the intransigence of Mr Gandhi. In 1945, with the advent of the Labour Government and the conclusion of the Japanese War, the time was ripe for action. I was the Prime Minister at the time, and I sent out a Cabinet Mission, of Sir Stafford Cripps, Mr A. V. Alexander, and Mr Pethick-Lawrence, the Secretary of State for India, and throughout the whole hot-weather season they worked with the greatest devotion to try to get agreement on the next step in progress towards full self-government. Communal tension had risen higher, and the Moslems and their leader, Mr Jinnah, were now demanding a partition of India between the provinces predominantly Moslem and those predominantly Hindu. The Labour Government considered that further delay would only make for greater difficulties, and it was accordingly decided that there should be a time limit after which the British would leave India, handing over to whatever Government or Governments could be formed. Lord Mountbatten, who had been extremely successful in dealing with troops drawn from many different races when he was Supreme Commander in South-East Asia, was appointed as Viceroy. Largely owing to his personal qualities and to those of his wife, and to the constant pressure of the time-table, eventually agreement was reached. Unfortunately this was done only by insisting on a division of India into India and

Pakistan. When this was agreed to by the Hindu and Moslem leaders the British Government reluctantly accepted it.

In the summer of 1947 British rule ceased in India. British troops withdrew, handing over to an Indian Army that now had fully qualified officers of high rank. The parting took place with the greatest possible amity between British and Indians, but was followed by a terrible outburst of communal violence in the Punjab. India became fully self-governing and was represented at the next conference of Commonwealth Prime Ministers. I had the honour of introducing into the House of Commons the Independence of India Act. But there was then a further possibility: should India stay in the Commonwealth or become completely independent? This question faced India and Pakistan. Very wisely, I think, both decided to stay in. But a further question arose as to whether it was possible for a member of the Commonwealth to become a republic. Hitherto one of the strongest bonds uniting the members of the Commonwealth had been a common allegiance to the Crown. India decided to become a republic, and the question of whether this was a possibility arose. It was fully discussed at a conference of Prime Ministers, who unanimously agreed to recommend to the King that India should still remain in the Commonwealth. The old title of Emperor of India would go by the board, and in its place would be a new title, Head of the Commonwealth. A new precedent was made on this occasion, when all the Prime Ministers waited on the King and gave him their collective advice.

Two tragic events occurred soon after the new regimes were installed. Mr Gandhi was murdered by a Hindu, and the Prime Minister of Pakistan, a wise statesman, Mr Liaquat Ali Khan, was murdered by a Moslem.

In the years that have passed India has made great progress and has carried out free elections on the largest scale on record. Pakistan has had a certain amount of teething troubles. The new Indian Government managed to induce the princes to surrender their sovereignty, although there were difficult incidents, particularly in Hyderabad and in one of the Gujerat states. But the greatest difficulty of all arose from the position of Kashmir, where a Hindu rajah ruled a predominantly Moslem people. Despite endless discussions, this has not yet been settled and still remains a bone of contention. It is remarkable that in India today there are more British civilians than ever before, and there are more than 100,000 Indians in Britain. In India, too, so far from endeavouring to root out every memory of the former regime, the Indians have accepted the best that Britain gave to them and stand out today as the leaders in the contest of democracy against absolutism.

During these years India has been fortunate in having as Prime Minister a very great man, Mr Jawaharlal Nehru. Educated in Britain, a devoted follower of Mr Gandhi, he has the qualities required for the difficult period of inaugurating this great change. In particular, by his wise toleration he has set a great example to the world.

Burma had been overrun by the Japanese, and only after a hard struggle were the Japanese driven out. Meanwhile some younger Burmans had been misguided enough to work with the Japanese. They were very soon disillusioned, and their young leader, Aung Sang, during the War made contact with General Slim and with Lord Mountbatten; they very wisely, realizing that these young men had been misled, accepted their offer to change sides and help in the War.

The future of Burma had now to be discussed. The Governor-General and the personnel of the old Burmese Government which had been in exile re-entered Burma, but the country was in very grave disorder; there were Communist bands hardly distinguishable from dacoits; there were troubles between the Burmese and the Karens, and of course there had been wide destruction of towns and communications. It appeared to the Labour Government that Burma, like India, must be given her full freedom, and a deputation of Burmese nationalists were invited over to Britain. They were at first very suspicious and were a little surprised when I told them that it was open to them to stay in the Commonwealth or achieve complete independence. It was unfortunate that on the return of the deputation from Britain their leader and most of his Cabinet were murdered. Fortunately the prompt action of the British Governor dealt with the murderer and restored order, but the Government fell into perhaps less-experienced hands, and Burma decided to become a republic and leave the Commonwealth. I think very likely if Aung Sang had lived matters might have turned out differently. Meanwhile, despite a good deal of trouble from Communists and dacoits and also Chinese troops, the Government of Burma has functioned, and at the time of writing General Ne Win, who was given rather wide powers to pull together a disorderly situation, has handed back power to the leading statesman, U Nu.

The big island of Ceylon attained full dominion status without any serious difficulties. A Commission had recommended government by a kind of committee system, but generally speaking it is found that fancy systems don't go down with Asians, who believe that the Westminster model is the only real one for democrats. I recall suggesting to Indians when I was over there on the Simon Commission that perhaps they would find the American presidential system more suited to their conditions, but they rejected it with great emphasis. I had the feeling that they thought I was offering them margarine instead of butter. In Ceylon there is also a communal question because of the large number of Tamils from South India who have been brought into Ceylon. And while the island made a very good start under the wise rule of Senanayake, there have been subsequent difficulties, together with the murder of a Prime Minister.

Farther East since the War great progress has been made. The great island of Singapore offered a particularly difficult problem, because, although part of Malaya, it had a majority of Chinese, and there is the question of how far the Chinese might be attracted to Communist China. However, self-government has been introduced and is functioning well.

There were similar difficulties in Malaya, where Chinese and Indian labour have been introduced, and the Malays feel an ever-present danger that they may be pushed out of their own country by these immigrants. There was a long and difficult campaign to overcome Communist Chinese who had taken to the jungle. Malaya was formerly under the rule of her own native princes, but with the march of time the rulers have now accepted their position in the Federation of Malaya, and the Prime Minister of Malaya attended the last Commonwealth Conference.

Borneo, part of which was formerly administered by a company and part of it by a white rajah, is probably too small to make a viable unit. It is possible that it might in time join Malaya and Singapore, which would avert the danger of a Chinese majority which now prevents a federation in that region.

The problem of the very small countries is extremely difficult. One cannot deny their right to self-government, but they cannot expect to have a full establishment which they cannot afford. In Asia there are Aden, Mauritius and Hong Kong and a number of smaller islands, not one of which is really self-supporting, and it is one of the problems of the Commonwealth to decide just what to do with them. Meanwhile it is well to note that Australia tends to take the lead in the Far East. She already has a mandate for some British possessions, as has New Zealand, and it may be that the future of the Pacific islands will be bound up more with Australia and New Zealand than with Great Britain.

Asia today is a critical battle-ground between rival

Ideologies, with China on the one side and India on the other as the chief protagonists. All democracies have a vital interest in the struggle. India is facing great difficulties, which she is seeking to solve by democratic methods, and she deserves all the help the Western world can give.

IV

Before dealing with the problems of Africa it is worth noting the development of self-government by Africans overseas in the Caribbean. The Africans there were, of course, imported as slaves, and with the abolition of slavery in the early years of the nineteenth century the islands in the Caribbean were governed paternally by Europeans. Three of those islands, Bermuda, Barbados, and Bahamas, had enjoyed a measure of self-government from the days of Oliver Cromwell, much the same kind of self-government in fact as was enjoyed by the American colonies. But the Africans had no share in the government. It was, of course, obvious that in due time the majority population of these islands would claim their rights. One of the difficulties was the very small size of most of the islands in the Caribbean and, before the advent of air travel, the wide spaces that separated them. I remember many years ago being struck by the number of Governors, Chief Justices, and Attorney Generals knocking about in these small communities, and it seemed to me that sooner or later there should be a federation. When I was Prime Minister I set on foot inquiries to this end, and today there is full domestic self-government in the islands and a Federation has been set up, but it is not yet certain that it will endure. Inevitably there is a certain rivalry between the major constituents of the group, Jamaica, Trinidad, and Barbados, but so far constitutional advance has proceeded very smoothly. The West Indies is fortunate in having a number of exceptional people and highly educated leaders. There is one possible danger, and that is the somewhat precarious economic conditions. Much depends on the price of a few commodities. But the Federation is now just ready to take its place as a full partner in the Commonwealth.

There are two neighbouring communities on the mainland, British Honduras and British Guiana, neither of which is either large enough or wealthy enough to sustain complete independence. We had hoped that these might join the Caribbean Federation, but at the present time they are holding off.

As I have stated, the wave of nationalist sentiment so strong in Europe in the nineteenth century took a long time to travel to Asia, and our Asiatic dependencies had a long period of apprenticeship. It has come, however, far more rapidly to Africa. There are even today comparatively few educated Africans. Many of them live under most primitive conditions. It is optimistic to expect any easy transference from a tribal organization to a democracy on the Westminster model. There are no old civilizations and no tradition of democratic government. There tends indeed to be a certain clash between the educated African of the towns and the old-fashioned tribal leaders. Up till quite recently British administrators tended to indirect rule through native chiefs, and where old-fashioned tribalism is eroded by the advent of Western cultures introduced by a minority there is bound to be difficulty.

45

In certain of the colonies such as Uganda there is not the problem of a considerable settled white community, but this obtains in Kenya, Rhodesia, and in its most acute form in the Union of South Africa. I have spoken already of the Union of South Africa as one of the old dominions, but when South Africa became a fully self-governing and free dominion the position of the Africans was hardly taken into account from the political standpoint. British and Afrikaners might have their differences, but they were for the most part at one in denying political rights to the Africans. But today in South Africa you have a double racial problem: there are first the differences between Afrikaner and Britisher, and secondly and more important is the problem of European and African. While Field Marshal Smuts was in power in South Africa, although the grievances of the African existed, they were not acute, but when Mr Malan succeeded, bringing with him the doctrine of apartheid, the trouble, formerly unobtrusive, came into the open. The fact is that while the rest of the Commonwealth has steadily proceeded towards greater and greater racial equality, the South African Dutch have seemed to go steadily back, and for many years now the Union of South Africa has been out of step with the rest of the Commonwealth.

In this lecture I can only note what is happening. It is not for me to prophesy as to the future. But as African state after African state becomes free it will be increasingly difficult for the European minority to hold their present position. It is also well to remember that in many parts of Africa, particularly in the East, the position is complicated by the presence of other minorities—Indians, Syrians, and the like. There is in Asia, particularly in India, a good deal of sympathy with awakening Africa; they do not always realize that to the African the Indian trader is as much an exploiting alien as is the European.

Within the Union of South Africa are three enclaves, Basutoland, Swaziland, and Bechuanaland. The Union has always coveted these and has put forward demands that they should pass to the Union. British Governments of every political colour have always denied this claim and have felt the responsibility of Britain for these African communities. Personally I would never have been prepared to concede to Mr Malan or his successors what was denied to General Botha and General Smuts. In these small enclaves there has been recently considerable progress, for the British Government realizes that to justify withholding them from South Africa their inhabitants must be given better conditions than those in the Union.

In Central Africa a very live problem is that of federation between Northern Rhodesia, Southern Rhodesia, and Nyasaland. Southern Rhodesia with a small white population has been given almost complete dominion status, and Northern Rhodesia has remained under the Colonial Office, as has Nyasaland. There are economic reasons in favour of federation, but in fact the great majority of Africans are against it. They see Southern Rhodesia too much like the Union. They would prefer, if they cannot get full independence, to remain under the Colonial Office. There seems a fairly hopeful outlook for political progress in Nyasaland, but this may lead to a demand for the rupture of Central African union.

One may note how under modern conditions events in one colony have repercussions in others. Africa can no longer be regarded as a number of separate dependencies in allegiance to various European nations, presenting essentially entirely separate problems. African nationalism is very much awake. What happens in the Union has its effect both in East and West Africa, while events in French Africa are known and considered by educated Africans all over the continent. At the present time it looks as if Ghana is likely to be the biggest influence on the peoples of the less-developed regions.

Most rapid progress has been made in the Western colonies. The Gold Coast, now called Ghana, with a vigorous Prime Minister in Mr Nkrumah, has already become a fully free and independent member of the Commonwealth, but it looks as if it may go the way of India and become a republic. Nigeria is just (May 1960) on the point of full dominion status. This is by far the largest and most populous of all the African colonies, but there are already difficulties there. From a distance one may think that there are just Africans on one side and Europeans on the other, but when European rule is removed all kinds of old enmities and ambitions break out again. It may well be not easy to reconcile these or to bring together in effective co-operation the chiefs of the interior and the educated Africans of the coast.

Sierra Leone, though a very small country and perhaps barely viable, is likely soon to follow the course taken by the other West African colonies.

In East Africa the position is complicated by the existence of a comparatively large European settled community. It may well be that more Colonial Office control in earlier days might have avoided some of the present troubles. One must note that already in Kenya there are difficulties between the tribes. The Masai, for instance, in old days were a warlike and conquering tribe, whereas others, such as the Kikuyu, were their victims. The troubles arising from Mau Mau have shown the gulf that exists between educated Africans and those who are only just emerging from primitive conditions. In East Africa also there are complications due to the existence of Indian and Syrian communities. These difficulties occur, but with a lesser acuteness, in Tanganyika.

One of the difficulties in Africa as contrasted with Asia is the small number of educated Africans and the lack of any background of indigenous civilization. I think too that it has not always been realized that in the small European communities such as Rhodesia and Kenya it is difficult to find European personnel qualified and able and willing to take on the responsibilities of government. Most Europeans are there in order to make a livelihood; there is no reservoir of leisured or professional people to form an adequate basis for parliamentary government.

One must then regard Africa as still in the stage of experiment, and it is too soon to judge whether the British form of democracy will prove acceptable. After

49

all, democracy is a very difficult system to work, and in Africa there is no tradition and the system is not really understood save by a very few Africans. There is a danger that when self-government comes democratic government may break down and dictatorships emerge. Over the years the United Nations, like its predecessor the League of Nations, was not very understanding of colonial problems; resolutions were apt to be passed by persons who had no real experience in administering backward territories.

It is now perhaps time to look at the position of the Commonwealth today. Clearly the difficulties increase with the membership. The kind of informal discussions which were so easy with four or five, or even seven or eight, Prime Ministers representing communities with more or less similar backgrounds, may well prove more difficult if the numbers of participants approach twenty. Numbers are always an important factor in the working of political institutions. I have explained in an earlier lecture the general way of working the Commonwealth, particularly its informality and its family atmosphere. What would happen if some units rejected democracy? One cannot imagine an autocratic government, whether communist or fascist, fitting easily into the framework of the Commonwealth. But a belief in and practice of democratic institutions is one of the binding ties in the Commonwealth. Formerly devotion to the throne was of the greatest importance, and is still so in countries such as Australia and New Zealand, but one cannot expect it to operate in Asian and African countries. Republicanism is a tradition of the Left, and much of the literature and the history of national movements tends to emphasize the republic as an essential feature of freedom, because these movements derive from the time when the revolutions of the Left were directed against tsars, emperors, and kings. In my view real democracy flourishes best under a constitutional monarchy such as obtains in Britain and Scandinavia; rather than in countries which, though apparently devoted to freedom and democracy and republicanism, suddenly lapse into dictatorship, as in South America. Another essential tie is acceptance of the rule of law. This does not mean a common code of law but that the local law is informed with the spirit of the British common law. Here one should not underrate the importance of the legal training in London of so many overseas statesmen. Yet another feature is the equality of citizens and personal freedom, but this does not obtain everywhere; the Union of South Africa is an outstanding example of failure to honour this principle. Then there is common interest: defence principles, trade principles. But there has never been and is unlikely to be anything of the nature of an imperial *zollverein*; this dream of Joseph Chamberlain passed away, and the most that has been done in uniting the Commonwealth has been the system of imperial preferences.

Generally speaking, one of the most important links between peoples physically separated is a common language, but there are a great number of languages in the Commonwealth, and the most one can expect may be that English, where not the first, should always be the second language. Nationalist movements not unnaturally tend to try to strengthen or even resurrect what is considered to be their own individual language; one can see this in Wales, where although Welsh is only spoken by a minority, there is a strong insistence on bilingualism in all persons appointed to positions of authority. In Eire great efforts have been made to revive the Irish language; the streets in the towns are given Irish names alongside the English, though I gather the former are seldom used. There has also been an attempt to make the younger generation speak Irish —I gather that has not been a very great success; I found myself that in Western Ireland where the children were forced to learn it in school they promptly proceeded to forget it as soon as possible, which is exactly what one would have expected in an attempt to force the Irish people to do anything that they did not specially desire. In Asia and Africa English is likely to continue to be the official language. In India an attempt has been made to make Hindi the official language for the whole of the peninsula, but this has roused great opposition from the speakers of Telugu, Tamil, Kanarese, Malayalam, and in fact, if India is to take the place that she should in Asia, she must retain English as a second language, for English, either in the British or the American form, has become the *lingua franca* of Asia. I recall a few years ago taking part in an Asian socialist conference which was also attended by some Africans, and I found all the participants speaking admirable English with the exception of one Japanese fraction, whose opponents most obligingly translated for them, and one French fraternal delegate, who spoke nothing but French.

Common culture? There is something in that as well. One finds it easy to discuss literature with educated Indians and Africans because they have absorbed a great deal of British culture. A common foreign policy? No. Even while still a member of the Commonwealth, Eire asserted its right to neutrality in the Second World War, and recently India has tended to hold aloof from the defence organizations, such as Seato, and to try to hold a middle position, though in view of aggression from China this is not very likely to continue. There is, however, still, despite the apparent fragility of these ties, a very real family feeling. I have travelled quite a lot in recent years, and where I met Commonwealth representatives I found family feeling very strong. Recently in a university in the United States of America I found that one of the professors had established a centre for Commonwealth students, and I met there at a reception in my honour students from Africa, Asia, Europe, and Canada, and there was a very delightful atmosphere.

One further rather curious link in the Commonwealth must be mentioned, and that is the game of cricket. Apart from a team in Holland and a couple in the United States of America, the game of cricket is confined to the Commonwealth, and with the exception of Canada, where climate stands in the way, it is played with enormous enthusiasm in India, Pakistan, the West Indies, South Africa, Australia, and New Zealand. Everywhere this very distinctive British game evokes

53

enthusiasm. Perhaps this last point may serve to emphasize the very peculiar character of the British Commonwealth of Nations; perhaps also it illustrates the difficulty to the foreigner of understanding its nature.

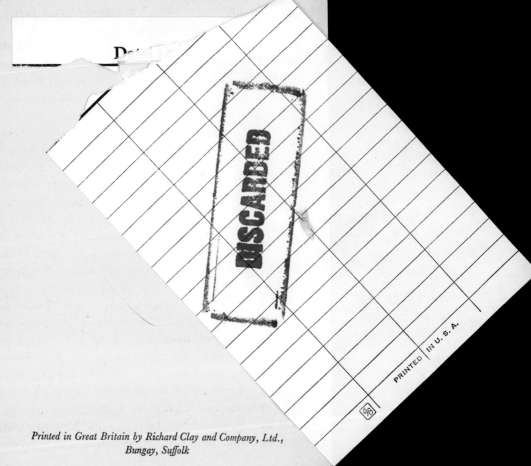

Printed in Great Britain by Richard Clay and Company, Ltd.,
Bungay, Suffolk